HOLD YOUR HEAD UP YOUR SELF-ESTEEM MATTERS!

BY

ESSIE A SULLIVAN

The contents of this work, including, but not limited to, the accuracy of events, people, and places depicted; opinions expressed; permission to used previously published materials included; and any advice given or actions advocated are solely the responsibility of the author, who assumes all liability for said work and indemnifies the publisher against any claims stemming from publication of the work.

All Rights Reserved

Copyright © 2023 by Essie A. Sullivan

No part of this book may be reproduced or transmitted in any form or by any means, electronic or mechanical, including photocopying, recording, or by any information storage and retrieval system, without permission in writing from the copyright owner. The views expressed in this work are solely those of the author and do not necessarily reflect the views of the publisher, and the publisher disclaims any responsibility for them. Any people depicted in stock imagery provided by Getty Images are models, such images are being used for illustrative purposes only.

Proisle Publishing Services LLC

39-67 58th Street, 1st floor

Woodside, NY 11377, USA

Phone: (+1 646-480-0129)

info@proislepublishing.com

ISBN: 978-1-960224-97-2

Contents

Dedication ii
Acknowledgments iii

CHAPTER 1
　Hold Your Head Up Your Self-Esteem Matters! 1

CHAPTER 2
　Childhood, Teenager, Adult life 3

CHAPTER 3
　How Self-Esteem was lost spiritually? 14

CHAPTER 4
　God has loved me first! 18

CHAPTER 5
　Mother Accepted Christ When I Was Around Twelve Years Old 24

CHAPTER 6
　Married At Age Twenty Years Old 30

CHAPTER 7
　Trouble In The Marriage—Divorced 32

CHAPTER 8
　I Raised A Teenaged Daughter And Two Baby Boys With God's Help 38

CHAPTER 9
　I Remained Single And Earned A Master's Degree In Business Administration With A Concentration IN Accounting 41

CHAPTER 10
　I Know Who I Am Now In Christ Jesus! 45

About the Author 48

Dedication

I dedicate this book to my late parents: Essie Mae Hughey and John Henry Hughey and my late grandparents: Essie Belle Wideman (affectionately "Bea") and John Henry Wideman – I loved you dearly! Thank you for everything you have done for me and that I have learned.

This book is written to all women, locally, nationally, and internationally and across the globe, especially to those who find themselves in a situation that you need to begin again and you can!

Acknowledgments

I would like to acknowledge my LORD and Savior Jesus Christ first of all for my Salvation and the finished work that he has performed on Calvary's Cross for me so I could hold my head up and understand that my self-esteem matters, and it matters to him above all for His great love for me (Amen)! Also, I would like to acknowledge my lovely dear sister in Christ, Henrietta Freeman, who so eloquently encouraged me to write this book on self-esteem. Mrs. Freeman invited me to a women luncheon at one of the local restaurants on a Saturday afternoon about three years ago. And at the luncheon, I along with the other ladies, was discussing self-esteem, and I shared with the ladies that I was important because I know who I am in Christ. I also shared that they were important as well because they are an original and not a carbon copy of no one, and no one has their fingerprint and that they are so important that God sent Jesus, His only Beloved Son, to Die for them to be restored to God through the shed blood of Jesus and that

He took their sins (this also included a low self-esteem that could be transformed in a healthy self-esteem). Thus, I would like to acknowledge my dear friend and friends for their support over the years that have prayed and encouraged me through the years. I would like to acknowledge Johnnie my dear baby sister, who is my rock, confidant, and encourager, and her family, affectionately Rotunda Lakisha—my niece who is more like my very own daughter, and Jesse, my kind handsome brother, and my other set of siblings (sisters/brother).

Overall, I would like to acknowledge my dearest three lovely children that the Lord allowed my husband and I to come together to bless us. God always have a purpose and plan for our lives. And He has a purpose and plan for your life.

CHAPTER 1

HOLD YOUR HEAD UP YOUR SELF-ESTEEM MATTERS!

Hold Your Head Up Your Self-Esteem Matters is a true-life story about an African American young girl who grew into an adult with little or no self-esteem to believe in herself. She had to grow up faster than her peers because of the circumstances of the family. And the choices she made based upon how she felt about herself and the values she held for herself. Her childhood, adolescent, teen, and adult life played a major role in the events of how from childhood to adult created struggles, determination, perseverance, low self-esteem, falling, getting back up, loving yourself, and you can always start again. And above all, you can start all over with Christ Jesus as your Personal Savior and Lord. I hope you will enjoy reading this personal memoir of Hold Your Head Up Your Self-Esteem Matters! Overall, if there is a will, then the human spirit cannot be denied, and self-esteem will rise because you are indeed fearfully and wonderfully made in Christ Jesus' Love!

CHAPTER 2

CHILDHOOD, TEENAGER, ADULT LIFE

In today's society, a woman's self-esteem is very important to her especially when there are very few voices to tell her. Self-Esteem is the core values, belief system, if you will, that a person feels about himself or herself and/or confident in oneself, ability, character, and self-worth. "Simply put, self-esteem refers to how you feel about yourself, says Dr. Shana Feibel, a psychiatrist at The Linder Center of Hope and the University of Cincinnati." http://www.healthline.com "She also describes self-esteem as your enduring perception of your qualities, abilities and characteristics; while self-confident refers to your belief in your own capabilities or the knowledge that you have the skills to navigate a particular task or situation; and self-worth describes your perception of your own value and worthiness as a person. Generally speaking, high self-worth means you view yourself as valuable and worthy of respect, loving and belonging." http://www.healthline.com.

However, I did not feel like that I had the above qualities of a healthy self-esteem about myself. I had struggled with low self-esteem for many years from a young child and through-out most of my adult life. I always felt inferior and less than in myself and abilities to accomplish those things that I felt was important to me. As Dr. Lindner has said that "a lack of self-esteem, however, can affect your both confidence in your abilities and your self-worth." http://www.healthline.com.

I believe that self-esteem is an epidemic, and everyone thinks about this subject from time to time.

Self-Esteem is a value that I am very passionate about in appreciating who you are. Therefore, through the Power of God the Father, God the Son, and God the Holy Spirit, I am writing on this subject of self-esteem. This subject as self-esteem will be specifically to women. I am writing on this particular subject of self-esteem because I once suffered from a very low self-esteem! I did not know how to love "Essie" and what it really meant to love and care about me. I thought that meant finding my worth and value through someone else to validate me. Little did I know that this was totally wrong thinking that I had received into my life from my upbringing as a young child to an adult.

To begin with my story goes like this. I will start from my childhood, connect the dots as I go along so you can keep up with me, teenager, and then into an adult. In my childhood, I grew up as a young child as much as I can remember with my mom and dad until I was about four or five years old. And then all of this changed because my mom, me, my brother and my sister moved in with my grandfather and grandmother because my dad did not create a godly home for us as a family so we could stay together! My father did things to make sure that my mom and we could not stay with him. He turned out to be a very different man. And as a result of this with my mom and dad being separated (back then you did not get a divorce), my mom began to develop mental sickness (I could not understand this until I was an adult) that I believed started to create some of my low self-esteem. By my mom and dad not staying together and now my mom being sickly most of my life that I can remember, I always hated my dad because he caused my mom to be sick because she loved him so much and wanted so much to be with him and for our family to stay together. (She took her marriage vows very serious and did not believe in remarriage and held onto the belief that her husband was her husband until death parted them, and my mom held onto this belief until my dad died.) Being the oldest child, I watched this hurt grow, and my mother's life was never the same.

Secondly, as a young child, my mother depended on me for so many things domestically concerning the house. I learned early on by my grandmother how to get up every morning and help with breakfast before going to school. And after school, I would come back home and cook the family supper for my mom, brother, sister, along with my grandmother. Then, after supper, we washed dishes, and I would do my homework. I was always encouraged by my grandmother to get my schoolwork done, and of course my mother would help me when she was able and felt good to help me. I know that my mother loved us with all her heart.

I remember one year that she bought me, my brother, and sister, all three of us, a pretty bike for Christmas, and of course, this was when my mother was working a restaurant job and she was able to do this for us. I always felt hurt because we did not have a mom and dad both that could provide and do things for us...however, they did what they could do...and I am thankful. My mom, me, brother, and sister all shared one room together, and my sister and I shared the same bed. As a result of this, I always said that "when I am on my own, that I was having my own room." I often wondered what it was like to have my very own room and not have to share a bed. Also, I believed that my low self-esteem grew more because my dad was away from us (and I knew that he was not coming home again), and he did not provide for us financially although my mom had him placed on child support. He halfheartedly paid it or not at all. This was also a putdown to my self-esteem.

Thirdly, I was ashamed that my mom was sick and others of my peers know about it and sometime they would make fun of how my mom would smoke her cigarettes (she smoked before the LORD took the taste out of her mouth). This made me feel different, damaged, and putdown. Sometimes I felt like I did not have parents to support me and nurture me and tell me how it was okay and that they were doing the best they could for me especially when other children would laugh at us or I knew that they were teasing me at school or on the bus. But I knew that my mom loved me. All I had ever wanted was for my mom and dad, brother, sister, and I to live under one roof together so I could have a mom and dad and we function as a family. As a result, this never happened again since my mother and father separated. This was a hurt that I always carried—especially throughout my teen years. I always thought that if my dad lived with me that he would buy me a bedroom suite, and I would not have to work and pay for it. But this was not true because my "father" was an alcoholic as well as an abusive person. He would have drunk up his money and family money and would not have bought me no such thing as a beautiful bedroom suite. Do not get me wrong. I still loved my father. He just did not have anyone to show him the importance or the correct way to care or do things for his family.

And as a teen, although my mother had four sisters and one brother, and she was #5 of the sisters (oldest of six siblings), I did not see stable men in three of my Aunt's lives; they were unfaithful men who were not good to them—these men were more so like boyfriends, and my aunts' self-esteem and self-worth did not mean much. They were not taught to love themselves. Most of the time, these men were abusive to them. You see, my aunts, especially two of them were more like my sisters, and people even would call them my sisters that did not know us. I loved my aunts, and they helped support me as well.

Now as I progressed along as a teen having so many responsibilities, my mother, sister, and I had the opportunity to move out of my grandmother's house to our own one-bedroom house. In doing so, I had to manage the finances to keep everything going—I had to grow up quick and had to play the role as a mother to my mother (I became the parent to my parent). She became so dependent upon me as though

I was her godchild. I always loved my mom and prayed for her to be well. My mother's illness was a big part of my life, and I felt like that the illness prevented my mother from becoming all she wanted to be or needed to be for always thinking about my daddy or her husband—as a person thinketh in his or her heart so is he or she (Proverbs 23:7a, KJV, paraphrased). Our thoughts rule our world and determine what negative or positive things will manifest in our world. This is why I never liked sickness. And I always said in my mind that I would not serve a broken-down, sick, pitiful God who could not do anything for me to help me to be well or at least be better. Nevertheless, I prayed that Mother would be well. She thought of her husband her whole life until he died. Mother felt bound to live with her husband even in her mind although he never returned for us as a family. However, like my mom, I always was hopeful that he would return for us. Then I had to come to the realization of understanding that the enemy comes to steal, kill, and destroy (St. John 10:10, KJV, paraphrased) (relationships) as many of the minds of individuals to keep the individual away or distracted from God so there is no focused attention on God but woe is me. Oh my God! Satan is a liar! Our Heavenly Father has defeated these pack of lies through his beautiful, divine Holy Truth that I am fearfully and wonderfully made marvelous are thy work and my soul knoweth right well (Psalms 139:14, KJV). And self-esteem is important!

My mom and I shared a lot and talked extensively about her dreams as follows:

1. She always wanted to go to New York City—the Big Apple!
2. She wanted to work in a bank to cash checks.
3. She always wanted to be with her husband and her thoughts were that she had a living husband, he was not by any means living and thinking about us.

This is the reason why that it is so vitally important that you place your "worth" and "values" in Christ Jesus because the mind of man is apt to go astray and live his own way especially if he does not have that strong male figure—biblical foundational principle of the LORD embedded in him regarding the importance of the family and his God-given role as a husband, role model, financial provided (breadwinner), and protector of the family. Husbands have a high calling in the LORD to do his will. However, if young male children are not taught these truths early on, then the enemy has an opportunity to lead and entice them in darkness by keeping them ignorant of God's truth, but thanks be to God the Father, God the Son, God the Holy Spirit that all power rest rules and abide over all! Thank the LORD for God's gifted prayer warriors that God has raised up to stand in the GAP for the redemption of these husbands' souls. They can change, and God continue working on their souls for change in Him! Amen!

Nevertheless, my dad did not come back home. God allowed us to make it through to the other side of what was not a favorable situation, and God allowed it to still work for us in a favorable way. However, this affected my self-esteem and contributed to my having a low self-esteem of myself. My dad left me! He left his family and did not look back! Oh my goodness, what a sad reality for such a young child! With this reality, I had to grow up fast and that maturity has helped me throughout my adult life—I was always ahead of my time or my youth if you please. In middle school and high school, when students are into different extracurriculars for afterschool programs and sports, I was at home cooking, making sure that my mom was taking her medicine right, cleaning the house, making sure that we had resources such as coals (woodburning stove for heat) and a good way to heat the house and finances were in place to last from one month to the next. As a result of this, we were approved for supplemental assistances such as food stamps and a check because we were too young to hold down a real job at this time—"Nay in all these things, we are more than conquerors through Him that loved us" (Romans 8:37, KJV).

CHAPTER 3

HOW SELF-ESTEEM WAS LOST SPIRITUALLY?

In being whole as a person in one's self-esteem means that we must know who we are in Christ Jesus. First, in order to know who we are, we must have a personal relationship with Him, as our known Savior and Lord. Secondly, in order for us to even be aware of our need to have a great spiritual self-esteem, we must know to have a great spiritual self-esteem, and we must know that sin separates us from God. This means that we, as the human race, were born into sin because of Adam. Adam is the first man that God created in the beautiful Garden of Eden—(Genesis 2:7, KJV). However, God made Adam perfect in every way and in every sense of the Word as God made him in the image of His Likeness. Therefore, in the creative state, God knew that Adam did not need to be alone; therefore, He caused a deep sleep to fall upon Adam (I believe this is why in real-time surgery, humans are given anesthesia and become unconscious when having surgery, so they don't remember the pain—also I believe this is where the first original doctor's occupation was born), and from Adam's rib, God used it to make woman, and (as you noticed that the word woman has man listed to complete the word woman) without the man, there would be no woman! The man plays a very important role in first things first to God as the head and leader of the woman.

Why we are born into sin is because Adam decided to disobey God and eat the forbidden fruit that Eve (his wife) had given to him.

God told Adam:

"And the LORD God commanded the man saying, Of every tree of the garden thou mayest freely eat: But the tree of the knowledge of good and evil, thou shalt not eat of it: for in the day that thou eatest thereof thou shalt surely die" (Genesis 2:16-17, KJV).

The enemy also told Eve:

"For God doth know that in the day ye eat thereof, then your eyes shall be opened, and ye shall be as gods, knowing good and evil" (Genesis 3:5, KVJ).

Eve was enticed by the enemy to eat from the Tree of Knowledge. She shared with Adam (her husband) and, as a result, sin entered the entire Human race because this was a direct violation to what God told Adam not to do! This caused the entire human race to be separated from God spiritually and now man does not have direct access to God—The Human Race is now spiritually dead and needs a Savior—Self-Esteem no longer exist after this act of Adam's disobedience to God.

"And the woman saw that the tree was good for food, and that it was pleasant to the eyes, and a tree to be desired to make one wise, she took of the fruit thereof, and did eat, and gave also unto her husband with her; and he did eat. And the eyes of them both were opened, and they knew they were naked; and they sewed fig leaves together, and made themselves aprons" (Genesis 3:6-7, KJV).

Therefore, God reprimanded the man and woman and enemy (serpent) for each of their decisions for disobeying

Him—then sin had entered the entire Human race because of one man's decision which instituted the "fall" or the curse of sin (See Genesis 3:8-24, KJV). This certainly is how we lost our self-esteem spiritually!

CHAPTER 4

GOD HAS LOVED ME FIRST!

God, He has my best interest at Heart and His blessings bring no sorrow. I am so glad that God is not afraid, and He is not scared, so I don't have to be afraid and scare either because my Heavenly Father is a courageous warrior and so am I! Jesus is my best Friend.

LORD, your Holy Word is so rich, wealthy, and great till there's hardly room to receive it. I can only image your great goodness that You have in the Earth for me and others. God has taken the pain of my divorce and turned it into a beautiful portrait of Himself. Through the pain of a troubled marriage, I wanted to walk in the things of the LORD, and my spouse wanted to walk contrary to the things of the LORD, and this is where the conflict started that inevitably led to a divorce—this was a great putdown to my self-esteem. Life happens beyond what we understand sometimes.

Therefore, after the divorce, I was left to raise three children—two baby boys in diapers, and they were still sucking a bottle, along with a daughter that was in middle school. This was the scariest thing that I had ever done especially having to work full-time and raise three children alone. I did not know that God understood how to help me raise my children and do all the other things pertained to raising a family—but He did know! And he also know how to help you as well. After work, I picked up the boys from day care (private sitter's home—my daughter had learned to ride the bus to and from the middle school), came home, and cooked. We ate supper as a family (we were not a dysfunctional family, only a single family in the Lord), I washed my baby bottles, bathe the boys, and did a nightly devotion with the children from the Book of Psalms, KJV—I read the Psalms that was age appropriate for them. I also asked God to lead and guide me in what to read to my children. Sometimes, I would read the devotion from Isaiah 6, KJV, and also Philippians 4:7, 8, 13, and 19, KJV. I would read from the children Bible as well to do the devotion. We sang and prayed and had a good time with the devotions. I prayed and pleaded the Blood of Jesus's Protection over my three children, myself, house, car, property, and also for our neighbor, especially if neighbor had moved in, and they were not acting right or there was strange activities of gathering that were unusual. All I can tell you is that God is Good through all of this. God was sovereign! Amen!

I tell you that I was so nervous initially after the divorce took place because I had always said that I did not want to have any man's children, and the biological father was not in the home because I knew how hard it is to grow up wondering where my daddy is when I was a little girl and why he's not taking care of my mom, brother, sister, and me. This is a heavy emotional weigh of the mind, but God is Sovereign!

Through having to be alone, God showed me how the enemy had taken my thoughts and thoughts of my spouse and used them to pull down my self-esteem through unhealthy words and behaviors (I did not know that at the time that words had a profound effect on what they do to our souls or our inner person and how damaging this could be). I had allowed this low self-esteem to take place because I did not know that I had a low self-esteem of myself, but then I became even more aware when God showed me that I am fearfully and wonderfully made (Psalms 139:14, KJV) and that He love me Dearly and that God needed me and wanted me to know this and that now I know that I have liberty and freedom in Him for my self-esteem, and He went to the cross just for me and took the self-esteem issue so I could feel good, loving, caring, and accepting of me as a beautiful woman in (Him) Christ Jesus! Amen! And Amen!

Although I was scared to no end here through my divorce and singleness, all of a sudden with three children, a house note/insurance, car note/insurance, utility bills, credit cards, and all to take care of as I thought by myself (as I was used to having a second income—but God is Sovereign!) because I did not know God or that God could help me raise three children and do all the above. And perhaps there are some similarities that you are wondering if God can help you with or does, He even care, and the answer is YES, YES, YES! Indeed YES! He cares about your CARES! Amen! He delights in showing you just how much He cares and loves you! Yes, You! He will provide everything that is needed, but you must trust Him to take good care of you and your children (now he is the unseen husband) and follow His Biblical principles, thus says the LORD. Amen! What are those principles?

Here are just a few that was most helpful to me to get you started:

1) I accepted Jesus as my personal Savior (Romans 10:9-10, KJV)—if you have never trusted Jesus as your savior to save your soul, then you want to acknowledge that you are spiritually separated from Christ because of your sins and must ask for forgiveness and ask Him to come into your life because he has already died and rose for you because He loved you so much!

2) I will accept the truth that God is Sovereign—He is Supreme over all!

3) I will do daily morning devotion for myself and at night with children if I am single or married, etc.

4) I will pray and seek God's power and strength over this situation (moving forward) and grow and learn from it.

5) God is my solid rock (all other ground is sinking sand)! He will not leave me and will not walk out on me and does not talk unkind to me. He loves me dearly. Amen!

CHAPTER 5

MOTHER ACCEPTED CHRIST WHEN I WAS AROUND TWELVE YEARS OLD

When I was around twelve years old, I remember my mom accepting Christ as her personal Savior. I know this to be true because we lived in a house within the Buncombe Street area in Greenville South Carolina. And during this time, this lady and her family moved like five houses down the street from ours. Little did I know that God was sending this lady to live on our street so she could witness to my mom about going to church and getting saved as accepting Jesus as her Personal Savior. Somehow, this lady befriended my mom, and she invited her to start going to Bible study with her. This went on for about a year with my mom going to church with this lady.

Then, the lady must have talked with my mom about me coming to Bible study and attending church with them. So, I did, and the next thing I knew is that I am at the Altar before the LORD asking Christ to come into my heart. The name of the church was Macedonia Fire Baptized Holiness Church in which I got saved. I was so glad that I accepted Christ. I was thirteen at the time, which would have been 1974. By accepting Christ and being in Church as a teenager, I believe God had the lady come to live on our street so He could for one deliver me from a world of sin. I had some Aunts, but some of them were more like my sisters rather than being Aunts that set godly example for me. It was quite the contrary. You see, God had a different plan for my life than what I knew to have for myself! Amen!

I walked with the LORD throughout High school, and He helped me tremendously. God indeed had a covering over my life, but He kept me from obviously getting in the different troubles and going down the wrong road that I would have originally would have been on. At this time, most of my life, we had lived with my grandmother, my mom, sister, brother, and myself. Grandmother had a significant other living in the same house with us. However, this is the reason why I would not suggest having an outside man living in your house if you are raising your children, and the man is not your children's biological father. This does not set up a good environment for your children and neither does it send a godly message to your children. It does nothing to build their self-esteem to let them know that they are important. As a matter of fact, this can be more harmful than good because trust me, if you have girls and an outside man living with you and them, believe me the enemy will suggest different things to the man about your girls because the enemy does not want your girls to serve the LORD at an early age but to keep them distracted from the truth of His Word. You, as a mother has to protect their innocence and cover them in the LORD. You are responsible for doing the right thing for your girls. They are precious and loved by the LORD and your sons as well. I am speaking about these things from a female perspective because I know how fresh an outside man will try to get with a young girl because it has happened to me. When an outside man lives in your house, especially if the man is not the father as I've said earlier, the man does not have the best interest in mind for your girls or children because the enemy always come with a different agenda to take you off the pathway of righteousness. Just be careful with your children as their self-esteem is important, and they need to hold their heads up too. However, on another note in reference to the above regarding an outside man, some men are not this way (in being used by the enemy) but have done an excellent job in raising step-children.

In changing the subject: during my High school years, my grandmother, mother, sister, brother, and I all attended the local community church. There, I was introduced to a gentleman who attended the local church as well. He was twenty-four at the time, and I was sixteen. Of course, he was too old for me to be seeing a twenty-four-year-old guy, but you would not know that he was twenty-four. He kept pursuing me during the evenings. When I went to my new church, Macedonia, he showed up there as well. After pursuing me for some time, he finally came to see my parents, which was my mom and grandmother, to ask if he could like me—I can remember as clear as day how nice, mannerable, kind, and what a perfect gentleman he was. I was so impressed with him—although he wanted to like me, my parents felt like he was too old. Now check this out. All I had ever seen growing up was the females in my family with older men. So what was modeled before me, I automatically chose an older man. Throughout my high school years for the eleventh to twelfth grade, I dated this older guy—at least sneaked and dated him because my parents were against me doing this (I wish that I had listened to my parents but I didn't…but my marriage provided me three beautiful children that I cherish) But when the influence is there to treat you like a queen and make you feel so fine as me being a young woman that was raised without the love of a father from five years old on into teen years, and when he came along, I was so easily swayed by his influence. Especially with him being older, I thought that he knew everything. He had a car and a job. He was polite, kind, giving, and supportive of me. I was so caught up into him because this man was so good to me. He did things for me. He proposed to me on Paris Mountain to ask me to marry him. I could not believe it! I was so in love with this man. I even loved the ground he walked on. Although my parents did not approve of him seeing me, eventually they did come around because we were married when I was twenty years old.

CHAPTER 6

MARRIED AT AGE TWENTY YEARS OLD

After graduating from high school at eighteen, a year later, I moved out of my mother's house to start keeping house of my own. This was the first time I had been on my own in an apartment. My mom did not approve of my boyfriend coming to see me and did not care for me to go out with him. Well, with his influence and growing up without a father, as I have said earlier, I moved out of my mom's house because I did not want to disrespect her, and I knew how she felt about me seeing this man.

However, at the age of twenty, he and I were married at my church, Macedonia Fire Baptized Holiness Church. There we had such a beautiful wedding, and I was so pleased with how things turned out that day. The only one issue that I had coming down the aisle is that my new husband to be did not acknowledge me coming down the aisle but looked down the whole time as I was escorted down the aisle by a very distinguished elderly gentleman that stood in the place of my father. I was not sure what this meant, but it was a little bit hurtful to me. I just could not understand that. I knew that my biological father would not come to give me away because I did not grow up with him, and by this time, he already had another family, so I knew that he would not come.

Sometime things can become so confused and complex to deal with—especially the important things of life. All of this contributed to my self-esteem being low as well. I did not even know that I had a low self-esteem but did not feel as good about myself.

CHAPTER 7

TROUBLE IN THE MARRIAGE—DIVORCED

From our upbringing regarding our childhood and into our adult years, we bring that little boy or little girl into the relationship of marriage with all of these expectations from the way we were raised, not realizing that he or she, meaning the husband or wife, cannot be who your father or mother raised you to be. Therefore, since we do bring a whole lot of baggage into the marriage, then we have to learn to revisit those childhood thoughts to overcome negative patterns, and we transfer those negative thoughts to our spouse. This is easily done than said. For example: I was raised with family members that did not trust the man to do as he said he would—and they had reason to not trust, which was acceptable, especially when an individual does not have the integrity to do what they said they would do. However, I grew up not trusting a man, so it was easy to transfer those negative thoughts to my husband, not realizing those seeds were from my childhood upbringing. He also transferred his childhood upbringing to me due to being domineering and talking down to me as though I did not know anything.

Therefore, this brought out the fussy attitude in me as a result of my childhood upbringing—this is how I understood to solve the issues. Little did I know that this created more issues due to this negative way of thinking. As a result of the above along with other issues that will not be discussed, I experienced a divorce after eighteen years of marriage. I just decided that I would not put up with a man that was unfaithful. I thought that at one time our marriage was very solid and stable, but when a person's mind is made up to go on their way, there is nothing you can do about how someone else thinks and how they view you and themselves or their decision. Just let them go! It is best in the long run because now you might need to heal emotionally, which is understandable. Be willing to do all you can, the best you can in your marriage for your spouse as it is reasonable. However, be sure not to violate your conscience. God never expects or intend for you to do anything contrary to what you should not do. This is so important. Sometimes the enemy comes in different fashions and forms even in the closest people to us. I am here to let you know for certain and for sure that God does heal even after a divorce. Because He loves you dearly and your dependence is in Him and Him along your Solid Rock—the Anchor Holds! (Psalms 18:2 KJV), Amen!

You might not be facing a divorce or have gone through a divorce; it might be something totally different. I am still here to tell you that God does understand you and your situation, and He is ready to help you at any moment when you ask Him to. He is always available to support you and take care of you because He knows the emotion of it, and it is too much for you to carry. I know this because I was once in your shoes! I know how you feel! But I am still here to tell you that there is help and support for you—this is not the end! This is a new beginning to start again with Jesus Christ! I do not know if you have a relationship with Jesus Christ or not, but you can at this moment.

You can pray the Sinner prayer:

Dear Lord Jesus, I am a sinner and I have sinned against a Holy God, and I am sorry, and I asked your forgiveness of my sins. I believe that you shed your precious blood and died on the cross for me to save my soul. I believe that you rose from the dead the third day and has ascended into Heaven and seated on the right hand of the Father. And I thank you for saving my soul. Romans Chapter 10, verses 9 and 10, KJV, states "That if thou shalt confess with thy mouth the Lord Jesus, and shalt believe in thine heart that God raised him from the dead, thou shalt be saved." "For with the heart man believeth unto righteousness; and with the mouth confession is made unto salvation."

Also, now you can ask Jesus, who is now your Savior, Best Friend, Confidant, and Your ALL in ALL, to take away the pain, and He will heal you of that hurt and also heal all your emotions. You say, how do you know? Well, I have been in a similar if not the same situation or valley as you have been in, and I am here right now at this moment to tell you Jesus is a Healer for you. He is so concerned about you, and He wanted me to let you know through this book. Jesus knows all about brokenness and hurt because He loved you so much that He has experienced that pain you are feeling on the cross in which he died for you and me and the whole entire world. You see, Jesus is so Awesome! If you prayed the above prayer and asked Jesus to come into your life, please write to me at email readthered12@gmail.com to share your blessing of receiving Christ as your personal savior.

Also, I am sharing this for encouragement that I have suffered with Postpartum Depression (PPD) (baby blues as a new Mother) after giving birth to one of my children. I thought that if I could not deliver a baby vaginally that I was less than a woman and that also affected how I felt about myself. I thought that my husband and I would witness me having a vaginal baby. However, I had to learn that having a baby vaginally is not what to focus on, but rather that God had given me a beautiful curly head, normal healthy baby and I was happy and this was what matter! I learned that Postpartum Depression was nothing to be ashamed of! My Heavenly Father God was very faithful and provided great medical care, guidance and support through my husband

and our church family, my family, and his family, for my complete Healing and I never suffered with PPD with giving birth to the rest of my children…God is more than Good! I am very thankful to those that were there for me and my family during this time.

Postpartum occurs after giving birth. According to the website "www.marchofdimes.org" article Healthy Moms Strong Babies…What causes Postpartum Depression (PPD)? We are not exactly sure what causes PPD, It can happen to any woman after having a baby. One possible cause that was interesting in the article as follows: Changing hormone levels after pregnancy. Hormones are chemicals in your body. Some help control your emotions and mood. During pregnancy, your body has higher levels of the hormone's estrogen and progesterone. But in the first 24 hours after giving birth, these hormones quickly go back to their normal levels. Therefore, this rapid drop in hormone levels may lead to PPD.

CHAPTER 8

I RAISED A TEENAGED DAUGHTER AND TWO BABY BOYS WITH GOD'S HELP

Well, some may say that a single woman cannot raise healthy, productive, godly citizens to make a contribution to the World's good. I am here to tell you for certain and for sure it can be done! We were only a single family and not a dysfunctional family—children believe what you tell them. I always built my children up and spoke blessings over them and told them that they were great and that they are important and that I am raising them to be good, godly, productive citizens to make a contribution to the World's good. And today, my dear, sweet, beautiful daughter is very successful with her family and in her career. She is now thirty-seven years old—she is a beautiful, young Christian woman in the LORD, and she blesses her husband and her family. To God Be the Glory! Now my eldest son is also very successful in earning an Electronic Engineering degree in

April 2018. He is a super young man! He loves the LORD and have a heart for the LORD. My youngest son decided to serve our Country as a dedicated citizen of the United States of America. He is very successful, and we thank him for serving and "Salute" him for his service. He also has a heart for the LORD. Amen! Thus, I have taught my children to love and respect us as parents because our decisions had nothing to do with them regarding going our separate ways. Needless-to-say, all three accepted Jesus Christ as their personal savior in their growing-up years. I raised them to be concerned and focused on the things of Christ to make our lives better by having family nightly devotions—as stated earlier, we were a single family, not a dysfunctional family. All three children are highly successful. I drove my children to school and also my daughter to middle school, but when she went to high school, she rode the bus. We attended one of the local churches on a regular basis, Sunday morning service, Sunday night service, and Wednesday night Bible study, and other activities that the children were participating in. I enjoyed raising my children and being a mom and seeing God working in such amazing ways! As confirmation, God put this in my spirit: God says (small still voice) I am enough to help you, and I am all around you. I keep your dwelling place safe, and I am the High Tower that you run to (Psalms 91, KJV, paraphrased). Also, I am the living God that have enough for you. I AM THAT I AM! Amen! To God Be The Glory!

CHAPTER 9

I REMAINED SINGLE AND EARNED A MASTER'S DEGREE IN BUSINESS ADMINISTRATION WITH A CONCENTRATION IN ACCOUNTING

Although, sometimes in your struggles or unforeseen situations, you do not realize that there are opportunities hidden in the very struggle that empowers you to a life goal or an opportunity that you did not consider as being possible. What I mean by this, as I have dealt with being divorced, I knew that I had a goal of always wanting to have my MBA, which is my Master's In Business Administration. I was so afraid initially to start school as a full-time parent with a full-time job and full-time family. Needless to say, God always has a RAM in the bush. He sent my dearest friend of many, many years to encourage me to attend school. She would know exactly how to encourage me as she is a veteran teacher with a very prestigious Doctorate Degree in Leadership and Education. She has always had a great love for teaching students and adults. It has been her passion. Therefore, my friend helped me to see the light and purpose of pursuing this worthwhile lifelong goal to attend school. Was it easy, No, by no means, because I had to set time aside to attend night classes on campus as well as take some classes online that were not offered on campus. This meant that I had to sacrifice time to stay up late nights to write papers and do my due diligent in completing current and relative information regarding assigned topics by my Professors. Although I was afraid to start school, not knowing if I could pass the course material or do well as a student for being away from school so long. However, that did not matter because once I got started, it was such an enjoyable adventure to go to class and meet other fellow classmates just like myself that were pursuing their degree as well and attending night classes due to full-time job responsibilities and family obligations, but yet like myself, they had their goals set high to succeed at acquiring their Master's Degree. I went to school from 6:00 p.m. to 10:00 p.m. was it hard? Yes, especially when a paper was due, and I had to set up until 2:00 a.m. in the morning to research the material and do my homework. I was able to coordinate this by cooking meals the night before for my children, and my daughter was my support staff while I attended night school to better our finances so I could support us with a great income. And also to show other women regardless of the circumstances that you are faced with if there is a will, a passion for what you desire, then you will not be denied! I am a living witness to this! By God's grace, I graduated from Strayer University on August 8, 2015, at 10:00 am with a Master's in Business Administration and I concentrated in Accounting. The commencement ceremony was at the Time Warner Cable Arena in Charlotte, North Carolina. I was so excited that this very day had come for me to walk across the stage and receive my degree! This was such an honor for me, and a lifelong dream had come true! I was just so excited to have my daughter (her daughter), my two sons, my sister (her daughter), and my sister's husband, my dearest friend of more than twenty years that has her doctorate degree, and two of my business associates attended my graduation as well. I was so blessed to have these family and friends as my support means so much—I cannot place a price on this, making family memories are so rewarding! This also helped in the rebuilding of my self-esteem in such a great way—now I knew that I had accomplished a dream that was on the back burner for so long, but God is faithful to his Word when we follow through in pursuing our goals. I am so proud of God's mercy and grace that saw me through this worthwhile goal. You might be wondering if you should go to school to pursue your master's degree or just go to school period or purse some other worthwhile goal—I am here to tell you that you can do it wholeheartedly if you have a desire or a passion. If I have accomplished this goal with all the required responsibilities in achieving my master's degree in business administration with a concentration in accounting, I know that you can accomplish your goal(s) with God's hand of support. He will definitely see you through to complete your goal. This may also possibly help give you more self-esteem or confidence to believe in yourself.

CHAPTER 10

I KNOW WHO I AM NOW IN CHRIST JESUS!

I am doing wonderfully well today, understanding who I am in Christ Jesus, and that I am fearfully and wonderfully made, and He, Jesus Christ, loves me dearly, and I am the apple of His eye (I am the center focus of His thoughts), and so are you! And because of Jesus, I hold my head up because my self-esteem is important.

Also, I prayed for my daddy's salvation when I had an opportunity to visit him in his home. He said that "he had accepted Christ and that he was sorry that he wasn't there for us, my mom, and the family, and that he did not intend or meant to hurt us, but he did, and I forgave him as well as my mom and myself. All is well regardless of my low self-esteem and how I felt, I still loved my parents and always will. They did the best they could, and I am grateful. We don't get to choose our family and set of circumstances. All I know is that God is faithful to us and get us through. And He can help you make it through too! In essence, God had provided love, healing, forgiveness, and transformation to help me to realize that I can hold my head up because my self-esteem matters and so does yours!

How to contact the Author for your Conference(s) listed below:

Author

Essie A. Sullivan, MBA

Evangelist License/Prayer Intercessor – November 19, 2017

By Pastors: Michael and Jennie Locke

Email: readthered12@gmail.com

About the Author

Essie A. Sullivan was born in Abbeville, South Carolina, and raised in Greenville, South Carolina. She is very passionate about women's self-esteem and believe that women are important in the way that they are treated or made to feel. However, women have come a long way in understanding the need to be understood and accepted for who they are as being important and needing to make a difference for our husband, children, careers, business, and church communities, and above all that God loves them dearly. This is her first book: Hold Your Head Up Your Self-Esteem Matters! It reveals that what God allow you to experience that if it does not call you home to be with him, He ultimately will use it for His Glory (nothing is lost, all is gained, Isaiah 61:3, King James Version) and bring you up as a blessing through it, and as a result—you become the blessing to many others because of it, and Christ is Honored.

Thus, Essie is a born-again believer in Christ Jesus, a mother of three beautiful children that she raised as a single devoted parent with the help of God. She has earned her Master's in Business Administration and concentrated in Accounting from Strayer University, School of Business, Greenville, South Carolina. She was licensed as an Evangelist and Prayer Intercessor via "We Are One In The Spirit Outreach Ministries," November 19, 2017. Thus, Essie enjoys sharing the Good News of Jesus Christ in reference to Salvation and Self-Esteem and how God can rebuild your Life.

Work Cited:

"Why Self-Esteem Matters refers to how you feel about yourself, says Dr. Shana Feibel, a psychiatrist at The Linder Center of Hope and the University of Cincinnati." <http://www.healthline.com>

"Signs Of Low Self-Esteem And What To Do: Dr. Joe Rubino, it is estimated that 85 percent of Americans suffer from low self-esteem…You are not alone if you are dealing with this issue." <http://www.betterhelp.com>

"Article: Postpartum Depression: Healthy Moms Strong Babies" <www.marchofdimes.org>

Do you have the desire to understand who you are and what makes you persevere to become greater? Having a low self-esteem can hinder you from achieving your dreams. It is vital to know that because we have an all-loving Father who created us in a realm of love that we can love ourselves. It is vital to know that Christ Jesus paid the price so that we can and will not let the circumstances of our lives hold us captive, and through Him we can do anything.

Essie Sullivan's Hold Your Head Up! Your Self-Esteem Matters unlocks keys to guide you through becoming a more significant you. Through her experiences of life, you will be able to grasp Bible-based principles that release you from the bondage of your past. She shares as an African-American female, she was able to overcome self-esteem barriers. In doing so, she conquered the stereotypes of being a divorced single parent. In rearing three children without a spouse in the home, she continued to trust in the Lord. Acquiring a Master's in Business Administration, she was able to be a role model her children needed.

Overall, this memoir allows you to understand that regardless of the pains from your childhood, adolescent, teenage, and adult years in living in a rut, you are fearfully and wonderfully made. That no matter how much you have striven to think more of yourself, you can know your beauty is found in the eye of your Creator. That mere man cannot provide you the inner release from captivity because you have the power through Christ Jesus to be alive unto God. You will discover that in forgiving others, you can have the power to love others. In so doing, you have the power to love yourself and overcome any obstacle.

Second book will be for men: You have a rightful place in Christ; you are somebody and honored!